WHERE ON EARTH AM I?

S. S. COULTER

Text and art copyright © 2023 by S. S. Coulter. All rights reserved.
Published in the United States by Good God Productions, Carmel, IN.

Library of Congress Control Number: 2023920623

ISBN: 978-1-959568-00-1

SSCoulter.com

THIS BOOK BELONGS TO:

_____

THE FASSA TAILS SERIES

BOOK 1: WHERE ON EARTH AM I?

BOOK 2: ALLY CAT

BOOK 3: ROWLF!

BOOK 4: MY FAIR CAT

BOOK 5: THE EXTRA-ORDINARY SCIENTIST

BOOK 6: KING OF THE NEIGHBORHOOD

BOOK 7: YOU LUCKY DOG-CAT!

TO MUFASA (AKA FASSA)...

...the cat that inspired me to begin The Fassa Tails. I have yet to meet another personality quite like you. You were SO funny, SO dramatic, and SO full of love! You ALWAYS surprised me and made me laugh – I still laugh when I think about you now. I hope these books do justice in illustrating just how much an amazing imagination and – even more importantly – a big heart and a kind character can positively impact others. You will always be one of a kind...
FASSAHHHHHH!!

And to my husband, my family, and everyone who encourages me and my creativity, including our loving Father God – thank you!

To read *Where on Earth Am I?* with S. S. Coulter, please visit SSCoulter.com/Book1

Well, hello there, Person! How are you on this glorious day? You're feeling positively purrrfect,
I hope!

My name is Fassa...and these are the wondrous tales of my friends and me! Would you like to join us on an adventure?

If so...come along!

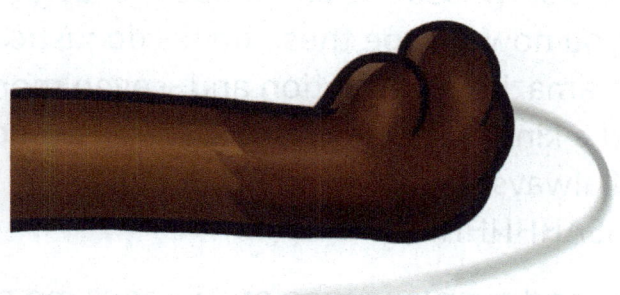

Inside you'll find tales of my friends and me.
Oh, the stuff we've done and the things you'll see!

Some adventures are short and others are long.
And on some we are scared, but on all we are strong.

So get ready, get set, and be sure to hold tight.
Because one thing's for sure – imagination's in sight!

Fassa woke up shivering. The last thing he remembered was lying helplessly in the snow while the pink-nosed cat was being driven away from him in a car. Now he was on a hard, dry surface, and the world felt like it was spinning around him in circles.

He slowly lifted his dizzy head to see where he was, but his eyelids were so heavy, he could hardly see through them. Squinting his green eyes, he could make out blurs of brown, red, white, and blue moving back and forth in front of him. He trembled and wondered, *Where on Earth am I?*

He lowered his head back down onto his big, brown paws and stayed as still as a statue. Whatever this mysterious place was, he didn't want any-*one* – or any-*thing* – to know he was awake.

Heavy eyes aren't enough to stop a cat like me! he thought. *I will use my fantastic feline ears to hear where I am!*

Fassa propped up his pointy, brown ears as far as they would go. He faced his right ear forward and turned his left ear crookedly to the side. Holding his breath, he concentrated on the sounds around him.

There were low rumbles...and some tapping here and there...and then click, clack, click, clack... some-*one* – or some-*thing* – seemed to be getting closer to him...and then BANG! BOOM! WHOOSH! Loud noises crashed into his ears from all directions.

Oh, my poor head! Fassa flinched and slammed his ears down flat.

In a moment, it was quiet again.

Fassa was, indeed, becoming frustrated. His eyes and ears, which were usually so reliable, had not helped at all. But he had to find that pink-nosed cat, so he wasn't going to give up! He thought about her bright pink nose and smiled. *I know! I'll use my sensational sense of smell!*

He pushed all the air from his lungs and belly out through his mouth. Then he shut his mouth and took a long, deep breath into his nostrils.

Uuuuck! he cringed as tons of smells rushed into his nose. Some he recognized — like those of other animals — but others were so yucky and strong that it felt like he could taste them!

His nose burned, his mouth watered, and his stomach twisted. He let out an awful cry:

"MRAAAAOHHHAH!"

Huffing and puffing, Fassa hoped no-*one* – or no-*thing* – had heard him. But he wasn't going to wait around to find out. *I am an amazing animal of action, and it's time I got out of here. The sights, sounds, and smells of this place may be purrrplexing, but they are no match for my long, leaping legs!*

He bent his elbows and knees, and scooched his legs under him. He would make his escape on the count of 3.

"Ooonnnneeee," he counted out slowly. "Twooooooooo," he breathed out for as long as his breath could go. "THREEEEEEEEEEE!"

Fassa leapt from the hard surface, expecting to sail through the air. Instead, he smashed into something cold and wiry and crashed right back down.

Shaking his head, his surroundings suddenly came into focus. Like magic, small, gray crisscrossing bars had appeared around him.

Fassa gasped. *Where on Earth did these come from?! Am I stuck inside a strange, small fence? Or worse,* his eyes bulged. *It's a cage!*

Living outside his whole life, Fassa had seen cages before, but he'd never been inside of one!

I'm trapped! Butterflies filled Fassa's stomach as his head became heavy again, his eyes blurred, and his whole body began to wobble like Jell-O.

Ohhhh nooo, Fassa moaned as he flopped onto his side. *Not THIS again!*

This was not the first time Fassa had gone all wiggly and ended up stuck on the ground where he'd rather not be…

The last time it happened, he was watching as a mysterious human had picked up his pink-nosed friend and put her into a car. Although the human was smiling, all he could see of his friend was her pink nose glaring at him through the car's window.

He wanted to go after her, but the sight of the unknown human scared him so much that instead of running, his body got as useless as it was now, and he toppled over into the snow.

He ended up just lying there helplessly while his friend was driven away from him.

Not THIS time! Fassa thought. *I will somehow get out of this cage, figure out where I am, and find my friend!* The corners of Fassa's mouth turned up and his chest puffed out. *I know! I'll use my crafty cat mind to control my wobbly body!*

Concentrating hard on moving his body, Fassa started by making his tail twitch. He then summoned his toes to wiggle, commanded his paws to stretch, and ordered his legs to flex.

Soon he was able to make his whole body obey him. He stood up onto his paws, ready to conquer any-*one* – or any-*thing* – that got in his way!

Looking out through the cage, Fassa could see the blurs of brown, red, white, and blue he'd seen earlier, but now they had formed into shapes. And they were shapes he knew: brown hair, red lips, a white coat, and blue pants.

Oh my! It's a human! Fassa gasped. *And it's looking right at me!* He slammed his eyes shut. *Brilliant! If I can't see it, then it can't see me.*

He kept his eyes closed and didn't move a whisker until he thought he heard the white-coated human walking away.

But when he opened his eyes, the human was still there, and it was walking toward him!

Fassa's legs started to wobble again…

NO! Stop THIS, cat! You need to show this human who's boss! Fassa glared at the human and hissed in his scariest, deepest voice. "I command you to back away." But the white-coated human ignored Fassa! Instead, it opened the cage door and reached toward him.

Fassa's teeth glared, his claws popped out, and his body vibrated with his giant growls. But as the human's hand landed on his back, it felt warm and calm. To Fassa's surprise, his body went from vibrating with angry growls to vibrating from happy purrs!

"Why, hello, sweet kitty-cat," the white-coated human said. "I'm your doctor. I'm so happy you're finally awake and even purring! And it's perfect timing too. There's someone here I want you to meet. I'll be right back!"

The doctor rushed away and was out of sight. But Fassa propped up his ears until he could make out her soft voice in the distance. She seemed to be talking to another human.

"Welcome back to the office," she said. "We have the tags for the cat you just rescued. I can't believe it, but just after you left this morning, a neighbor of yours brought in another stray cat. They found him almost frozen stiff in the snow."

"Oh no!" said another voice. "Is he ok?"

"He just woke up and seems to be doing fine. I thought you'd like to meet him!"

"Oh, I'd love to!" the second voice answered as they moved into Fassa's view. Wondering what could possibly happen next, Fassa nervously looked up at the mysterious, new human.

Her hazel eyes twinkled, her white teeth sparkled, and she spoke to him in the sweetest voice he'd ever heard. "Nice to meet you, handsome boy!"

Fassa's heart fluttered as she reached down to him. For a moment, he thought he might go wobbly again, but as she cuddled him into her soft arms, he felt more relaxed and safe than ever before.

What on Earth is happening? he thought.

"You know, Doctor, there's always room in our home for one more. I'd love to take him!"

"PPPPPUUUUUUUURRRRRRR!!!!" Fassa's purrs vibrated as loud as a freight train when he realized what had just happened – he finally was going to have a Person and a home of his very own!

As Fassa's new Person carried him out of the office, he thought nothing could possibly get any better. He looked up at her smiling face again, just to be sure it was all real. And at that moment, he realized there could be something even better! He recognized that smile. He was in the arms of the same smiling human he had seen driving away with the pink-nosed cat!

My purrrsistence has paid off, Fassa thought with a grin. Perhaps he would see his friend again...

Well, hello there again, my friend.
Don't worry – this is NOT the end!

More adventures are still yet to come.
And on each, we'll have so much fun!

I hope you'll join us in Book 2.
Who knows the things we will do!

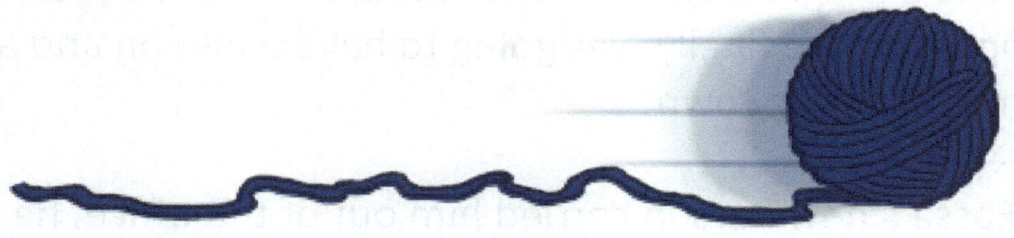

In the second story of The Fassa Tails series, **Ally Cat**, you may, indeed, learn more about the mysterious pink-nosed cat! You'll find a preview on page 60.

BUT FIRST...

...IT'S TIME FOR MORE FUN NOW!

To read *Where on Earth Am I?* with S. S. Coulter, please visit SSCoulter.com/Book1

On the following pages, you'll find:

- Plot Twists: 27-32

- Fun Activities: 33-44

- Hidden Pictures: 45-46

- Coloring Pages: 47-50

- A Word Search and Quiz: 51-54

- A Preview of Book 2, **Ally Cat:** 60-68

LET'S GO!

PLOT TWIST 1: IF AT FIRST YOU DON'T SUCCEED, TRY, TRY AGAIN

To read the Plot Twists with S. S. Coulter, please visit SSCoulter.com/Book1

HERE'S WHAT HAPPENED IN THE ORIGINAL STORY

Huffing and puffing, Fassa hoped no-*one* – or no-*thing* – had heard him. But he wasn't going to wait around to find out. *I am an amazing animal of action, and it's time I got out of here. The sights, sounds, and smells of this place may be purrrplexing, but they are no match for my long, leaping legs!*

He bent his elbows and knees, and scooched his legs under him. He would make his escape on the count of 3.

"Ooonnnneeee," he counted out slowly. "Twooooooooo," he breathed out for as long as his breath could go. "THREEEEEEEEEEE!"

As you know, Fassa kept trying until he met his Person!

BUT WHAT IF THIS HAPPENED?

Huffing and puffing, Fassa hoped no-*one* – or no-*thing* – had heard him. But he was tired and didn't feel like trying anymore.

His eyes, ears, and nose hadn't helped, and he decided he didn't want to try anymore. He laid his head on his paws and thought, *I give up!*

Uh oh! Things have gotten tough, and instead of continuing to try, Fassa decides to give up. If the doctor thinks he is still asleep, he may not meet his Person.

Sometimes when things are hard, we want to give up after just a few tries. The good news is that if we keep trying and don't give up, we can be a success – we can succeed!

Help Fassa keep trying until he succeeds by cheering him on. **Clap your hands, and yell out this helpful cheer: "Try, try again! Try, try again! Try, try again!"**

Great job! Now Fassa won't give up, and he will meet his Person.

ALWAYS REMEMBER!
IF AT FIRST YOU DON'T SUCCEED,
TRY, TRY AGAIN

PLOT TWIST 2: MIND OVER MATTER

HERE'S WHAT HAPPENED IN THE ORIGINAL STORY

Not THIS time! Fassa thought. *I will somehow get out of this cage, figure out where I am, and find my friend!* The corners of Fassa's mouth turned up and his chest puffed out. *I know! I'll use my crafty cat mind to control my wobbly body!*

Concentrating hard on moving his body, Fassa started by making his tail twitch. He then summoned his toes to wiggle, commanded his paws to stretch, and ordered his legs to flex.

Soon he was able to make his whole body obey him. He stood up onto his paws, ready to conquer any-*one* – or any-*thing* – that got in his way!

As you know, Fassa kept concentrating until he met his Person!

BUT WHAT IF THIS HAPPENED?

Fassa tried to make his body move, but he was having a hard time concentrating. He kept getting distracted by the things that had happened. What were the colors he'd seen earlier? What were the loud noises he'd heard? What was the yucky stuff he had smelled and tasted? And why was he in this cage? He just couldn't seem to focus, so he couldn't make his body listen to his mind.

Oh no! Fassa has gone through a lot, and he can't stop thinking about it. Instead of concentrating and standing up, he is stuck on the cage floor. If the doctor thinks he is still sick, he might miss out on meeting his Person.

Sometimes when we've had a bad day, it can be easy to think about all the bad stuff that has happened and get sad. That's when we want to use our "mind over matter" to stay focused on the good things and keep going!

Help Fassa stay on track by showing him he can use his mind to concentrate and stay focused no matter what is happening around him. **Focus and hold your breath while you blink your eyes 5 times.**

Good work! Now Fassa will keep concentrating until he meets his Person.

**ALWAYS REMEMBER!
MiND OVER MATTER**

ACTIVITY 1: 5 SENSES SCAVENGER HUNT

To do this activity with S. S. Coulter, please visit SSCoulter.com/Book1

WHAT YOU NEED
1. Paper or 5 Senses Chart (see page 35 or make your own)
2. Writing utensil

SUMMARY

Fassa was in a mysterious place and had to use his senses to figure out where he was. Now you get a turn to test your senses by going on a 5 Senses Scavenger Hunt. On the hunt, you'll use your 5 senses to find, describe, and draw things!

DIRECTIONS

1. Use your senses to find and describe the following things:
   a) **Sight:** Find something bright with a lot of colors.
   b) **Hearing:** Find something that makes loud or soft noises.
   c) **Touch:** Look for something that feels funny to your fingers. It could be soft, rough, or slippery.
   d) **Taste:** Imagine something to eat. How does it taste? Is it sweet, sour, salty, or just plain gross?
   e) **Smell:** Find something that smells interesting. It can be yummy smelling or yucky!

2. Fill out your 5 Senses Chart as you go. Describe or draw pictures about the objects you find. You will use your

descriptions or drawings later in a 5 Senses Guessing Game, so try to write down or draw tricky clues. Here is an example:

Sense	Item Found	Describe It
Taste	Popcorn	It is buttery and salty. It is the size of a marble. It is very light and easy to chew.

You can fill out the chart on the next page or make your own.

EXTRA CHALLENGES

1. Make another 5 Senses Chart! Use your 5 senses to find objects that are opposite of what you found the first time. For example, if you found something that tasted gross the first time, now find something that tastes sweet.

2. Play a 5 Senses Guessing Game! Find people who don't know what objects you found. For each item you found, tell them what sense you used to find it and then read them your description or show them the picture you drew, and see if they can guess what the item is.

THINGS TO TALK ABOUT

1. In the story, which senses did Fassa use to figure out where he was?

2. Think about how often you use your senses every day. Is it more than you thought?

3. What if you could not use one of your senses? What do you think that would be like?

5 SENSES CHART

Sense	Item Found	Describe It
Sight		
Hearing		

Sense	Item Found	Describe It
Touch		
Taste		
Smell		

ACTIVITY 2: FEAR NOT!

To do this activity with S. S. Coulter, please visit SSCoulter.com/Book1

WHAT YOU NEED
1. Coloring utensils
2. Paper

SUMMARY
Fassa was afraid when he was trapped in the cage and wasn't sure where he was. Have you ever been afraid of anything, like spiders or the dark? Make your fears less scary by drawing them and then making them look funny!

DIRECTIONS
1. Draw something you are afraid of.

2. Next, look at the picture and think about why you are afraid of it.

3. Now, draw something on your picture that makes it less scary or even funny! Here is an example of Fassa's fear made funny:

4. When you finish, hang your picture somewhere. Whenever you're afraid, look at your picture to help you feel better.

EXTRA CHALLENGE

Help others make their fears funny! Have others draw pictures of their fears, and then help them draw something on their pictures that will make them smile.

THiNGS TO TALK ABOUT

1. What did Fassa do to overcome his fears?

2. Is there someone or something you can think about to help you when you're afraid?

3. Even brave people are scared sometimes. Adults: talk about ways you have conquered your fears and share any advice you have.

ACTIVITY 3: BALANCING ACT

To do this activity with S. S. Coulter, please visit SSCoulter.com/Book1

WHAT YOU NEED
No supplies needed

SUMMARY
When Fassa found out he was in a cage, his body went all wiggly with fear. Then he used concentration to make his body move. Now it's your turn to concentrate and do a Balancing Act!

DIRECTIONS
See the Balancing Tips at the end of this activity for suggestions.

1. Stand in an area with plenty of room.

2. Lift your right foot off the ground and count to 20. Concentrate and try not to fall. Switch feet and count again.

3. Lift your right foot again, and now wiggle your toes 20 times without putting your foot down. Switch feet and try again.

4. If those were too easy, do 20 ankle circles on each side.

5. If that was easy, try doing the ankle circles with your eyes closed!

6. Now, lift your right leg and bend your right knee at a 90 degree angle in front of you. Count to 20 without putting your foot down. Switch knees and try again.

7. Next, try the same move from #6, but this time, stretch your arms straight out to your sides. Very slowly, one hand at a time, use your pointer fingers and touch your nose.

8. If that was easy, close your eyes and challenge yourself to stay balanced while trying to touch your nose!

9. Next, lift your right leg straight behind you and stretch out your arms like Superman. Slowly tilt your body downward and see if you can touch your toes without falling! Switch legs and try again.

EXTRA CHALLENGES

1. Have a Balance Competition with someone else using the balancing challenges you did in the Directions.

2. Try to think of other balancing challenges to do together.

THINGS TO TALK ABOUT

1. Just like Fassa had to concentrate to move his body, you had to concentrate so that you wouldn't fall down. Was it hard to concentrate?

2. Was it easier to balance on your right of left foot?

3. Was it easier to balance with your eyes open or closed?

4. Was it frustrating trying to keep from wiggling?

5. Did you try different ways to keep your balance? What did you do? What worked best?

6. Adults: explain to your kids that some things in life will take a lot of hard work, just like the Balancing Act. Consider sharing a story about a time when you worked hard to overcome a challenge. Describe how you kept your focus until you reached your goal.

BALANCiNG TiPS

1. Try to eliminate distractions before beginning.

2. Pick a spot in the room to focus on before and during the balancing challenge.

3. Hold for a less amount of time, and work your way up. Start with 5 seconds instead of 20.

4. Practice!

ACTIVITY 4: STARFISH STRETCH

To do this activity with S. S. Coulter, please visit SSCoulter.com/Book1

WHAT YOU NEED
No supplies needed

SUMMARY
When Fassa was held by his Person for the first time, he felt more relaxed than ever before. Now it's your turn to make your body feel relaxed!

DIRECTIONS
1. First, sit on the floor and try to make yourself into a ball by wrapping your arms around your knees.

2. Next, make your body tense by squeezing your entire body as hard as you can for 10 seconds.

3. Then, slowly let your body relax by letting your arms and legs stretch out onto the floor so that you look like a starfish.

4. Close your eyes and breathe in for 5 seconds, and then breathe out for 5 seconds.

5. Feel your muscles and body loosen up.

6. Take a few more deep breaths in and out, and feel good while you relax.

EXTRA CHALLENGE

Try doing something similar to this while standing up – so you can make your body relax when you are not at home and need to calm down. While you're standing, simply hug yourself tight and count to 10. Then, release your arms down by your sides while you breathe in for 5 seconds and then out for 5 seconds. Keep breathing slowly and feel your muscles and body relax.

THINGS TO TALK ABOUT

1. Were you surprised how it felt when you stopped squeezing your body and laid down on the floor? Did your muscles feel loose?

2. Did you like the feeling of being relaxed?

3. Are there times when you have felt tense that it would be helpful to make yourself relax?

ACTIVITY 5: FASSA TAIL TWISTER

To do this activity with S. S. Coulter, please visit SSCoulter.com/Book1

WHAT YOU NEED
No supplies needed

SUMMARY
See how well you can say Fassa's "tail-twisting" sentence!

DIRECTIONS
1. Say the tongue twister below slowly. Repeat it as many times as you need until you don't miss a word.

> Furry Fassa feels frightened facing feline fears, but Fassa finds his fears funny when a friend appears!

2. Next, try to say it as fast as you can.

3. Finally, see how many times you can say it in a row without missing a word!

EXTRA CHALLENGE
Try to come up with your own Fassa Tail Twister!

FIND THE HIDDEN PICTURES

Three of Fassa's favorite things are hidden in the story's illustrations: a sweater, popcorn, and Fassa's imaginary friend, Fred the Frog. Can you find them?* This is what they look like:

1. Where is the sweater hidden?

   ☐ Under Fassa, on a blanket

   ☐ On the wall

   ☐ In the car

2. Where is the popcorn hidden?
   - ☐ On Fassa's forehead
   - ☐ In Fassa's cage
   - ☐ On a cabinet

3. Where is Fred the Frog hidden?
   - ☐ On the car
   - ☐ In the snow
   - ☐ On the white-coated human

This is Fassa's imaginary friend, Fred the Frog. You can color him on page 50!

*Find the answers on page 55.

COLORING PAGES

It's time to color some of the story's illustrations – and Fred the Frog – just the way YOU like!

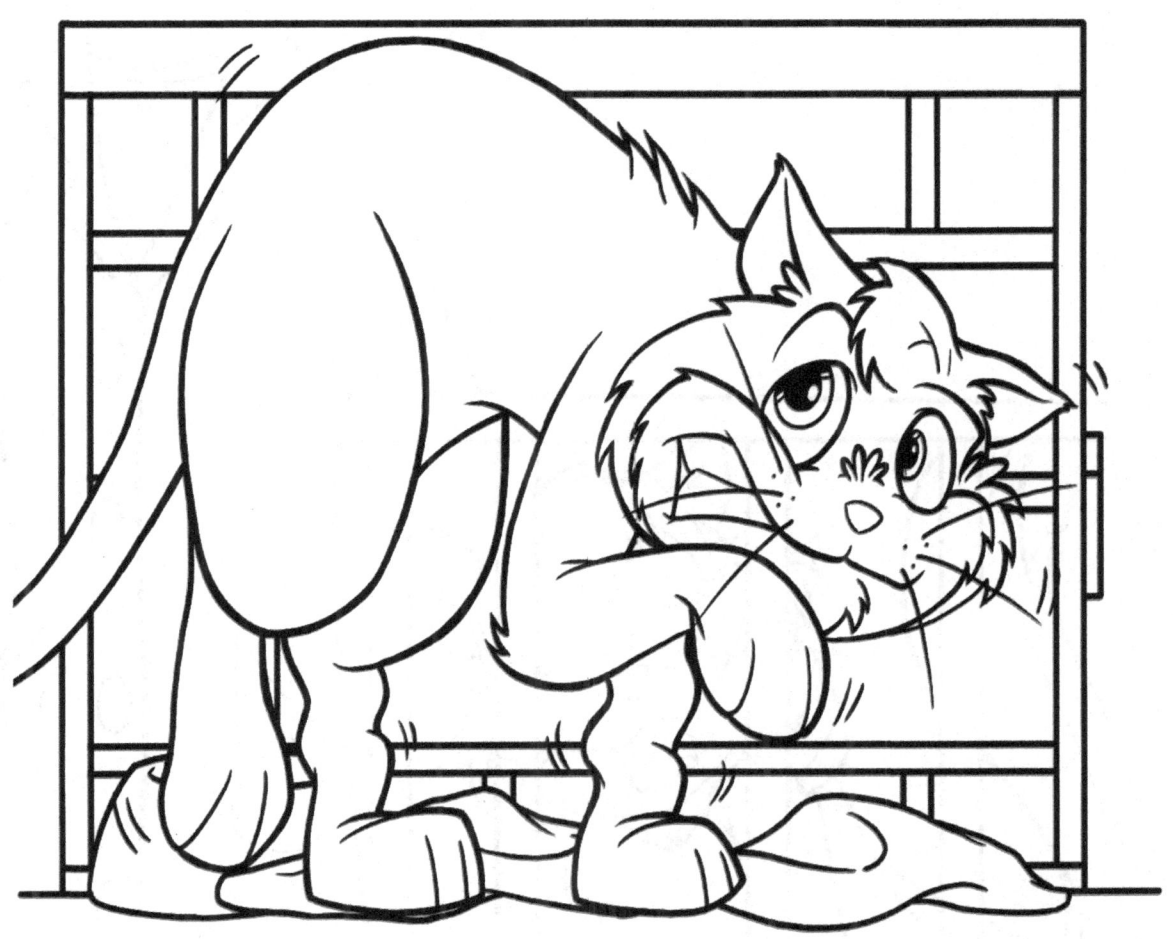

Please visit SSCoulter.com for Coloring Pages you can print out.

WORD QUIZ

It's time to see if you know some of the big words used in the story! Check your answers on page 56. Good luck!

1. Fassa **trembled** and wondered, *Where on Earth am I?* (Page 2)
   Tremble means:
   - ☐ Sit still because you are happy and calm
   - ☐ Shake because you are scared or cold

2. Whatever this **mysterious** place was, Fassa didn't want any-*one* – or any-*thing* – to know he was awake. (Page 4)
   Mysterious means:
   - ☐ Strange and you don't know much about it
   - ☐ Easy for everyone to see

3. Fassa **flinched** and slammed his ears down flat. (Page 6)
   Flinch means:
   - ☐ Stare off into space
   - ☐ Move quickly because something scares or surprises you

4. Fassa was, indeed, becoming **frustrated.** His eyes and ears, which were usually so reliable, had not helped at all. (Page 8)
Frustrated means:
- ☐ Feeling excited about what you are doing
- ☐ Upset because you are having a hard time solving a problem

5. Fassa was, indeed, becoming frustrated. His eyes and ears, which were usually so **reliable,** had not helped at all. (Page 8)
Reliable means:
- ☐ Good and trustworthy like your best friend
- ☐ Not very nice

6. Some smells Fassa **recognized** – like those of other animals – but others were so yucky and strong that it felt like he could taste them! (Page 8)
Recognize means:
- ☐ Know what something is
- ☐ Be surprised

7. *The sights, sounds, and smells of this place may be **perplexing**, but they are no match for my long, leaping legs!* Fassa thought. (Page 10)
   Perplexing means:
   - ☐ Easy to understand
   - ☐ Very confusing

8. **Concentrating** hard on moving his body, Fassa started by making his tail twitch. (Page 16)
   Concentrate means:
   - ☐ Forget about what you are doing
   - ☐ Make your brain think hard and focus

9. But the white-coated human **ignored** Fassa! (Page 20)
   Ignore means:
   - ☐ Really listen to what someone is saying
   - ☐ Do not pay attention to someone

10. *My **persistence** has paid off,* Fassa thought with a grin. Perhaps he would see his friend again... (Page 24)
    Persistence means:
    - ☐ Keep trying and don't give up
    - ☐ Try once and stop if it doesn't go your way

WORD SEARCH

Now see if you can find the 10 words from the Quiz in the Word Search below. Words can go in any direction and can share letters as they cross over each other. Check your answers on page 58. Have fun!

```
T O A X O F C M B F X G E U P
T R W N L S U Y O Y N N Z D E
D Z E I M R O S I I V B I K R
O B N M O P T T X V G P N Y S
P C G Z B D R E D Q L N G L I
H Q D U C L L R L F V J O I S
A G P W H P E I W B J F C R T
W L R N R D M O D D A A E Q E
L O M E L R C U D U S I R M N
O L P Q O J V S S W I D L S C
K J Q E T W K H E V N Q L E E
C V N P L H Y U L Q E J N A R
E Q L T C T X C S T L Q G U R
C O N C E N T R A T E D F K G
D E T A R T S U R F W A E J G
```

**TREMBLE   MYSTERIOUS   FLINCH   FRUSTRATED
RELIABLE   RECOGNIZE   PERPLEXING   CONCENTRATE
IGNORE   PERSISTENCE**

HiDDEN PiCTURES ANSWER KEY

1. Where is the sweater hidden?:

    ☐ **Under Fassa, on a blanket** (Page 11)

    ☐ On the wall

    ☐ In the car

2. Where is the popcorn hidden?

    ☐ On Fassa's forehead

    ☐ In Fassa's cage

    ☐ **On a cabinet** (Page 21)

3. Where is Fred the Frog hidden?

    ☐ On the car

    ☐ **In the snow** (Page 13)

    ☐ On the white-coated human

WORD QUIZ ANSWER KEY

1. **Tremble** means:
   - ☐ Sit still because you are happy and calm
   - ☐ **Shake because you are scared or cold**

2. **Mysterious** means:
   - ☐ **Strange and you don't know much about it**
   - ☐ Easy for everyone to see

3. **Flinch** means:
   - ☐ Stare off into space
   - ☐ **Move quickly because something scares or surprises you**

4. **Frustrated** means:
   - ☐ Feeling excited about what you are doing
   - ☐ **Upset because you are having a hard time solving a problem**

5. **Reliable** means:
   - ☐ **Good and trustworthy like your best friend**
   - ☐ Not very nice

6. **Recognize** means:
   - ☐ **Know what something is**
   - ☐ Be surprised

7. **Perplexing** means:
   - ☐ Easy to understand
   - ☐ **Very confusing**

8. **Concentrate** means:
   - ☐ Forget about what you are doing
   - ☐ **Make your brain think hard and focus**

9. **Ignore** means:
   - ☐ Really listen to what someone is saying
   - ☐ **Do not pay attention to someone**

10. **Persistence** means:
    - ☐ **Keep trying and don't give up**
    - ☐ Try once and stop if it doesn't go your way

WORD SEARCH ANSWER KEY

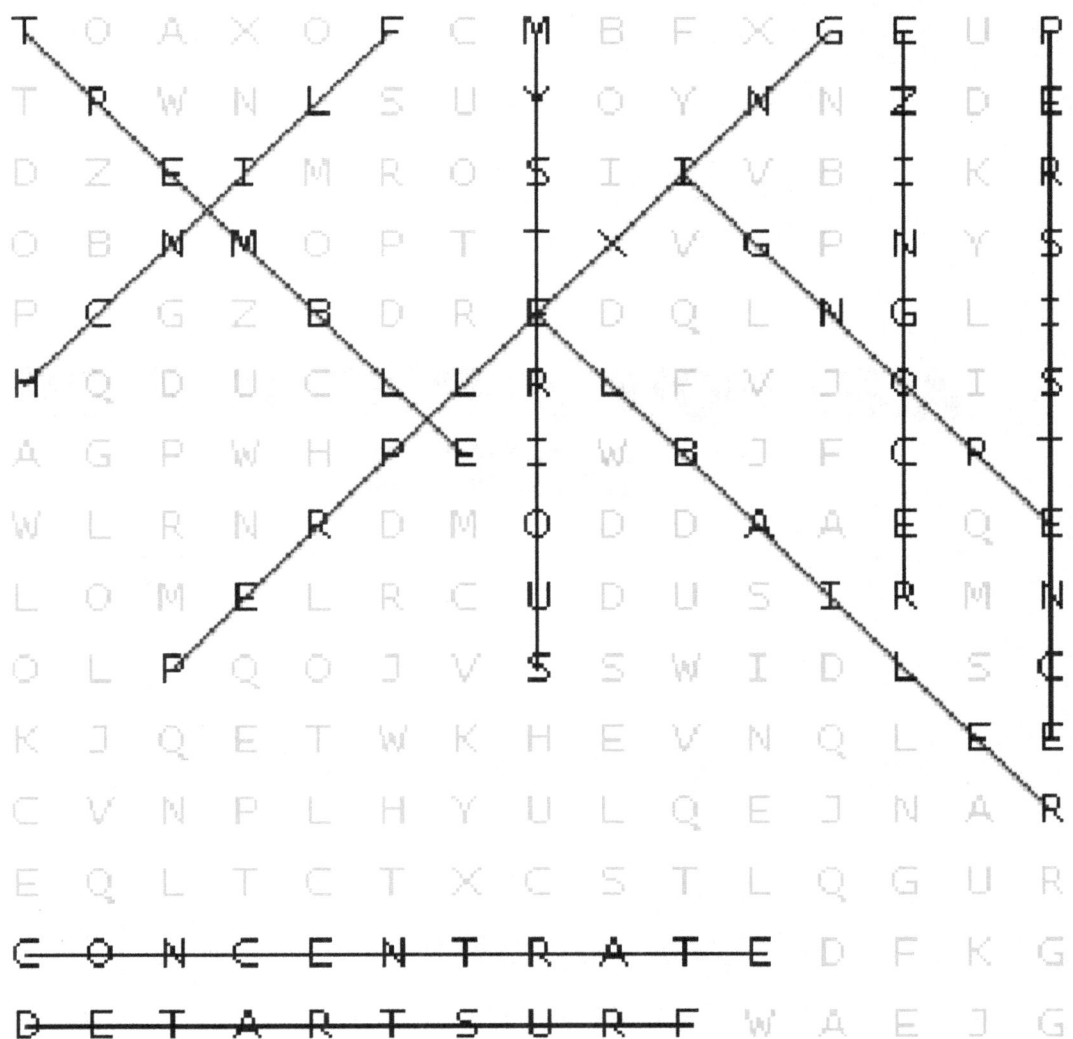

Please visit SSCoulter.com for Word Searches you can print out.

AND NOW A PREVIEW OF BOOK 2!

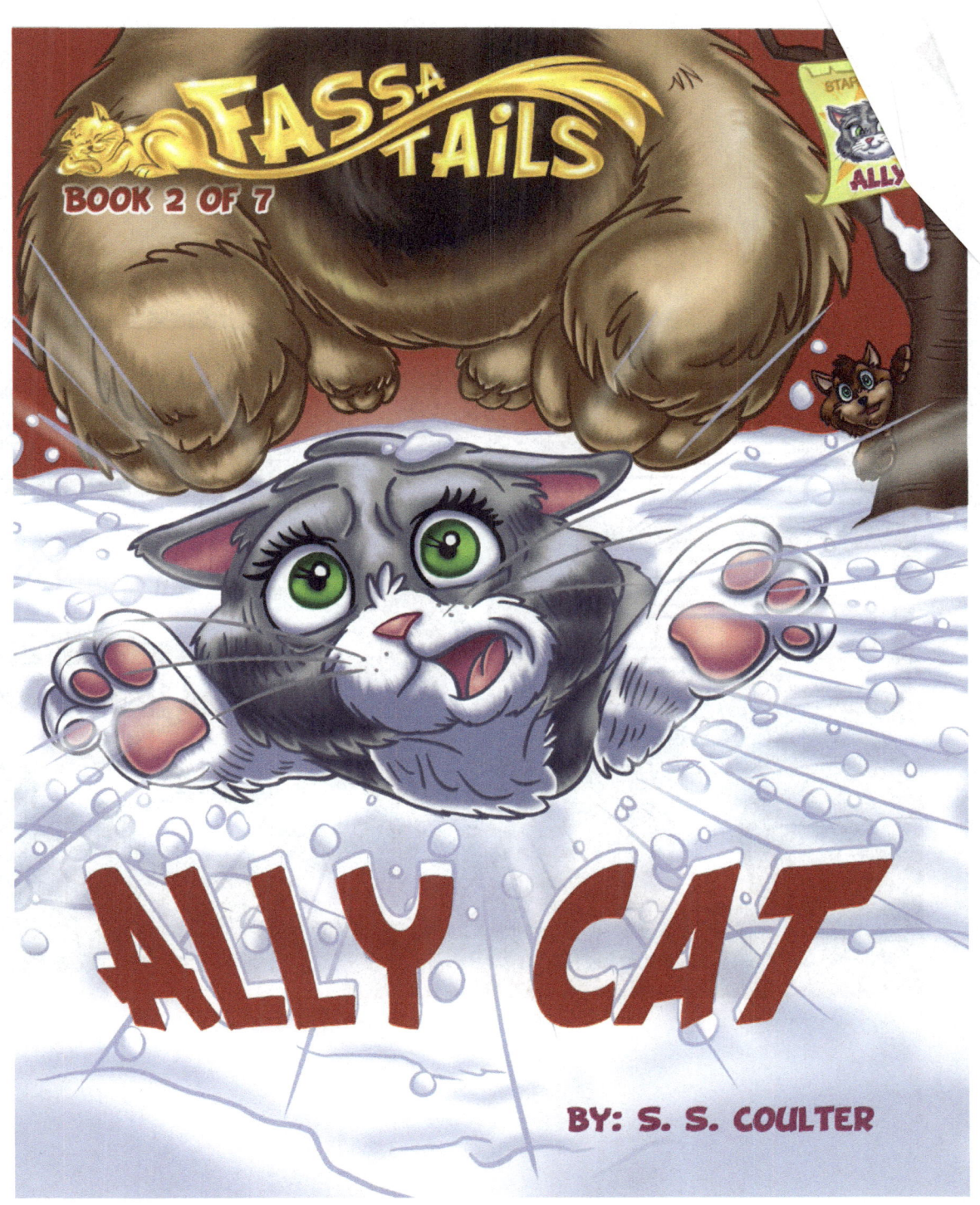

"Welcome home!" Fassa's new Person said as she pulled her car up to a lovely house with red bricks and green shutters. Looking through the window, Fassa realized he had seen this house before! He quickly paced back and forth along the car's back seats, almost certain the pink-nosed cat would be inside.

While he waited for what seemed like nine lives to be carried from the car, he pushed his nose against the rear window. The cold window stung his skin and reminded him of the first time he'd seen his pink-nosed friend...

WE NOW GO BACK IN FASSA'S MEMORY.

Not so long ago, before he woke up in the doctor's office, Fassa found himself wandering outside, lost and cold on a brisk wintery day. Snowflakes as big as cat paws danced back and forth as they made their way from high up in the clouds to the ground down below.

Fassa couldn't remember the last time he'd seen anybody, and all he could see now – in every direction – was white. His stomach growled with hunger, his paws stung from the cold, and his fur was heavy with sticky snow.

All of a sudden, through the thick blanket of white, a bright pink dot appeared in the distance. It zigzagged back and forth and bounced up and down. *What on Earth is that?* Fassa's eyes bulged.

He began to run toward it, trying to zigzag and bounce just like it did. But with each step, his fur became heavier with snow, and his legs could not carry him as fast as he wanted to go. *This will not do! I must show this sinister snow who's boss!*

He looked around him and grinned. *Brilliant! I will make like a snowball and roll!* He tucked his chin and dove into the snow. First went his head and his shoulders, then his back and his tail...over and over and round and round he went...until THUMP! Some-*one* – or some-*thing* – stopped him.

"HMMFPH! Ouch!" A muffled sound came from beneath him. Looking down, Fassa's eyes bulged again. He had landed right on top of the pink dot, and now he could see that it was no dot at all. It was a nose! And it was attached to a beautiful face, with whiskers and ears just like his.

In a daze, Fassa simply sat there, staring at the pink-nosed cat beneath him...

***

To find out what happens next,
please go to SSCoulter.com

THE ADVENTURES HAVE JUST BEGUN!

Please visit SSCoulter.com to find:

- **The entire Fassa Tails series.**
  In The Fassa Tails series, we follow Fassa as he uses his great imagination and kind heart to tackle obstacles and meet his best friends: Ally, Rocky, Angel, Cassie, Tubby, and Loki. Each book is filled with valuable life lessons in the story, which are then reinforced with pages of Bonus Activities – fun play ideas, plot twists, conversation starters, coloring pages, and more! The books are meant to be read in order, each ending with a cliffhanger that leads to another adventure!

- **Coloring Pages** and **Word Searches** you can print out.

- **More Activities** to make your day even better!

A BIG THANK YOU

Many people have helped along the path to creating this series and the activities that go along with it. Thank you to Kelly Kadlec and Errin Bald for dreaming up so many wonderful activities, and to Matt Mance, Robert Apolinar, and Robyn Bernd for helping bring the characters to life.

ALWAYS REMEMBER!

At times, things can get tough, and we can lose our focus or get scared thinking about the bad stuff that's happened to us. Sometimes we just want to quit! But if we can keep focused, keep trying, and keep ourselves from giving up, our hard work can really turn into great things...

- Persistence pays off!
- If at first you don't succeed, try, try again!
- Mind over matter!

For God hath not given us the spirit of fear; but of power, and of love, and of a sound mind. (2 Timothy 1:7, KJV)

ABOUT S. S. COULTER

Through The Fassa Tails and their activities, S. S. Coulter wants to spark kids' imaginations to help them more fully experience the joy of childhood. The idea is to jump start kids' creative juices to inspire hours of their own imaginative play and help them become aware of all the beautiful, cool, creative, and fun things that exist INSIDE of them – apart from technology and the other pressures of life. Ms. Coulter's childhood was filled with this imaginative play, which gave her fulfillment, peace, and joy – and she truly wants today's kids to experience the same thing!

Made in the USA
Las Vegas, NV
27 December 2024

15487511R00044